Study Guide

What Great Teachers Do *Differently*: Seventeen Things That Matter Most

Second Edition

Beth Whitaker and Todd Whitaker

Routledge
Taylor & Francis Group
New York London

First published 2012 by Eye On Education

Published 2013 by Routledge
711 Third Avenue, New York, NY 10017, USA
2 Park Square, Milton Park, Abingdon, Oxon OX14 4RN

Routledge is an imprint of the Taylor & Francis Group, an informa business

ISBN: 978-1-596-67205-5 (pbk)

Cover Designer: Dave Strauss, 3FoldDesign

Table of Contents

Introduction ix

Part One: Chapter 1: Why Look at Great?
Chapter 2: It's People, Not Programs 1
   Key Concepts 1
   Discussion Questions 2
   Journal Prompt 3
   Group Activities 4
      38 Years of Teaching Fifth Grade 4
      It's Not What You Do, It's How You Do It 4
   Application 5

Part Two: Chapter 3: The Power of Expectations 7
   Key Concepts 7
   Discussion Questions 8
   Journal Prompt 9
   Group Activities 10
      Stop the Thumping! 10
      Expectations, Rules, Consequences 10
   Application 10

Part Three: Chapter 4: If You Say Something, Mean It 11
   Key Concepts 11
   Discussion Questions 12
   Journal Prompt 13
   Group Activities 14
      Trust Me 14
      Calling All Parents 14
   Application 16

Part Four: Chapter 5: Prevention versus Revenge 17
   Key Concepts 17
   Discussion Questions 18

Journal Prompt 19
Group Activities 20
   A Bag of Tricks 20
   The Top Twenty 20
Application 21
   Discipline Practices Self-Assessment 21

Part Five: Chapter 6: High Expectations—for Whom?
Chapter 7: Who Is the Variable? **23**
Key Concepts 23
Discussion Questions 24
Journal Prompt 25
Group Activities 26
   Expectations—For Everyone 26
   Mission, Vision, Values 26
Application 27

Part Six: Chapter 8: Focus on Students First **29**
Key Concepts 29
Discussion Questions 30
Journal Prompt 31
Group Activities 32
   "Students First" Teachers 32
   Believing in Students 32
Application 34

Part Seven: Chapter 9: Ten Days Out of Ten **35**
Key Concepts 35
Discussion Questions 36
Journal Prompt 37
Group Activities 38
   The Power of Praise 38
   Our Cup Runneth Over! 38
Application 38

Part Eight: Chapter 10: Be the Filter **39**
Key Concepts 39
Discussion Questions 40
Journal Prompt 41

Group Activities 42
   Circle of Friends 42
   Filtering Out the Insignificant 42
Application 43

Part Nine: Chapter 11: Don't Need to Repair—Always Do Repair 45
Key Concepts 45
Discussion Questions 46
Journal Prompt 47
Group Activities 48
   The Builder 48
   A Restorative Approach 48
Application 49

Part Ten: Chapter 12: The Ability to Ignore **51**
Key Concepts 51
Discussion Questions 52
Journal Prompt 53
Group Activities 54
   Ignore and Intervene Pointers 54
   Acting It Out 55
Application 55

Part Eleven: Chapter 13: Random or Plandom?
Chapter 14: Base Every Decision on the Best People **57**
Key Concepts 57
Discussion Questions 58
Journal Prompt 59
Group Activities 60
   Graffiti on the Walls 60
   More Math Homework 60
   Random/Plandom 60
Application 61

Part Twelve: Chapter 15: In Every Situation, Ask Who
Is Most Comfortable and Who Is Least Comfortable **63**
Key Concepts 63
Discussion Questions 64
Journal Prompt 65

Group Activities 66
   Dear Parents 66
   Dealing with Difficult Parents 66
Application 67

Part Thirteen: Chapter 16: Put Yourself in Their Position **69**
Key Concepts 69
Discussion Questions 70
Journal Prompt 71
Group Activities 72
   The Student Perspective 72
   Understanding Student Behaviors and Responding Effectively 72
Application 73

Part Fourteen: Chapter 17: What About These
Darn Standardized Tests? **75**
Key Concepts 75
Discussion Questions 76
Journal Prompt 77
Group Activities 78
   Two Key Questions 78
   The Role of Standards 78
Application 79

Part Fifteen: Chapter 18: Make It Cool to Care
Chapter 19: Clarify Your Core **81**
Key Concepts 81
Discussion Questions 82
Journal Prompt 83
Group Activities 84
   Seventeen Things 84
   Clarifying Your Core 84
Application 84

Seventeen Things That Matter Most **85**

Introduction

This *Study Guide* is a tool to accompany the second edition of *What Great Teachers Do* Differently: *Seventeen Things That Matter Most* by Todd Whitaker. A practical resource for educators examining what great teachers do that sets them apart from others, this book focuses on the beliefs, behaviors, attitudes, and commitments that positively impact teaching and learning in our classrooms and our schools.

Note to Facilitators: If you are conducting a book study group, seminar, or professional development event, this *Study Guide* also serves as a road map to help you organize your sessions and work with your group. It provides assistance to staff developers, principals, team leaders, college professors, and other educational leaders who are working with teachers as they develop their professional skills.

What Great Teachers Do Differently: *Seventeen Things That Matter Most* is a slender, but powerful book. It is not a book comprised of hard scientific data, detailed assessment rubrics, or esoteric theories. Instead, it is a book that clearly, concisely, and accurately informs teachers what our most effective teachers do on a daily basis. Put simply, this text is a book that teachers can put to use—immediately. This guide, therefore, is written in a way that allows the participant not only to read and understand essential concepts, but also to take these back into their classrooms and schools and put them to immediate use.

Each part of this book corresponds to one or two chapters of *What Great Teachers Do* Differently. To help you plan and organize your study sessions, each part is divided into the following five sections:

- **Key Concepts**: These summaries of the key points of each chapter in the book will help you review and focus your thoughts.
- **Discussion Questions**: These questions and ideas help you learn more about yourself and your colleagues and will aid constructive conversation in the study group, workshop, or classroom setting.
- **Journal Prompt**: Based on the specific contents of each chapter, the journal prompts help you reflect, work through essential issues, and record what you have learned in writing.
- **Group Activities**: These activities allow you to explore concepts and ideas further by interacting with others in your study group, workshop, or classroom.
- **Application**: This section provides strategies for applying what you have learned in your school.

The authors would like to thank Jeff Zoul for his assistance in the preparation of these materials.

Part One

Chapter 1: Why Look at Great?
Chapter 2: It's People, Not Programs

🔑 Key Concepts

♦ Great teachers do not use sarcasm, yell at kids, or argue with students in front of their peers.

♦ Educators can always learn from observing what great teachers do. Eliminating inappropriate choices does not help as much as identifying good ideas used by successful educators.

♦ All that is truly needed to improve education is for *all* teachers to be like our very *best* teachers.

♦ *Who we are* as teachers and *what we do* as teachers are more important than what we know. Teachers must self-reflect on who they are and what they must do in order to improve their practice.

♦ There are really only two ways to improve any school: get better teachers and improve the teachers already there.

♦ No program inherently leads to school improvement. It is the people who implement sound programs who determine the success of the school. Programs are never the solution and they are never the problem.

♦ What matters most is not *what* teachers do (including "programs" such as whole language, assertive discipline, or open classrooms), but *how* appropriately and effectively they do it.

? Discussion Questions

1. What is the most important idea communicated in these two chapters? How would you implement this idea in your classroom?

2. Why should we look at what great teachers do?

3. In what ways is looking at ineffective teachers pointless? On the other hand, why must we also study less effective teachers and schools when determining what constitutes great teachers and schools?

4. What is it that determines—in the eyes of parents and students—whether or not a school is great?

5. Are open classrooms, back to basics, whole language, and assertive discipline programs inherently good or bad? Explain.

6. When considering whether or not to adopt a school program change, what should stand as the primary criterion?

7. In the phrase "poor lecturer's classroom," which of these three words captures the problem? How is this single example illustrative of the "people versus programs" concept?

Think of a program that has been implemented in recent years at your school or a school with which you are familiar. Which teachers adapted to the change of programs, embracing the new idea and making it work? Did any teachers resist the change? Was the program ultimately deemed a success? What determined whether or not it was successful?

_____

_____

_____

_____

_____

_____

_____

_____

_____

_____

_____

_____

_____

_____

_____

_____

_____

_____

_____

_____

_____

38 Years of Teaching Fifth Grade ...

In small groups of three to five, ask participants to consider the following two points: (1) Some teachers have twenty years of teaching experience; others who have taught for twenty years have one year of experience that they have repeated twenty times. (2) Students want to know how much you care before they care how much you know. On page 5 of the text, there is a description of a teacher who taught the same grade effectively for thirty-eight years. Have participants use the scenarios above and discuss how they apply to this particular teacher. Have groups create a list with three categories: *what she knew* as a teacher, *who she was* as a teacher, and *what she did* as a teacher. Based on the description of this effective veteran teacher, ask participants to brainstorm possible outcomes within each category that would likely have applied to her and her knowledge, passion, and practices as an educator. Participants should be prepared to share these lists with the entire group.

It's Not What You Do, It's How You Do It

Beginning on page 8 of the text, three "programs" are described that are deemed neither a problem nor a solution: open classrooms, assertive discipline, and lecturing. Participants should be divided into three groups. Ask each group to review one section of the text ("How Open Classrooms Got Started," "Assertive Discipline—the Problem or the Solution," and "The Poor Lecturer's Classroom"). Each group should then create and present a skit to the entire group showing how the program in question can be both an effective and an ineffective strategy in teaching.

Notes

✓ Application

In his book *Good to Great: Why Some Companies Make the Leap ... and Others Don't*, Jim Collins[1] maintains that good is actually the enemy of great. That is, the reason there are so few *great* companies is that so many people are willing to settle for *good* companies. He extends the examples to schools, indicating that the reason we have so few great schools is primarily that we have good schools. Whitaker's text, too, speaks to the shade of difference between good and great teachers, stating that most teachers do about as well as they know how. Maintaining anonymity, identify two teachers who are settling for good and two teachers who always strive for greatness. What is the obvious difference between the two pairs? Write your insights and reflect on what the great teachers are doing differently from those classified as merely "good." Share these observations at the next session.

Notes

---

[1]Collins, J. (2001). *Good to great: Why some companies make the leap ... and others don't.* New York, NY: HarperCollins.

Part Two

Chapter 3: The Power of Expectations

🔑 Key Concepts

- Great teachers focus on expectations; moderately effective teachers focus on rules; the least effective teachers focus on the consequences of breaking the rules.

- Great teachers establish clear expectations at the outset of the school year and follow them firmly, fairly, and consistently throughout the year.

- Rules have drawbacks, including the fact that they focus on undesirable behaviors. Expectations focus on desirable behaviors.

- Teachers may have varying expectations, but all great teachers set expectations that are clearly established, focused on the future, and consistently reinforced.

? Discussion Questions

1. What is the most important idea communicated in this chapter regarding teacher expectations?

2. What are the advantages and disadvantages of spelling out specific consequences for breaking rules?

3. What is, at times, a more powerful deterrent to misbehavior than a list of predetermined rules and consequences?

4. Why is it vitally important that teachers establish clear expectations at the beginning of the school year?

5. In addition to setting clear expectations for students each year, for whom else do great teachers set expectations each new school year?

Notes

✎ Journal Prompt

Take a moment to consider what is vitally important to you as a teacher in terms of managing your classroom and setting expectations so that your students learn and behave to the best of their ability and to your level of expectation. Decide on no more than three to five items and state these as expectations for students. Brainstorm in writing how you can communicate these expectations clearly, how you can ensure that they are consistently reinforced, and how you will respond when students fail to meet them.

_____

_____

_____

_____

_____

_____

_____

_____

_____

_____

_____

_____

_____

_____

_____

_____

_____

_____

_____

_____

Stop the Thumping!

On page 14 of the text, a scenario is described whereby the school principal only adds to the "problem" of thumping by announcing an edict regarding such behavior during the middle of an instructional period. In groups of five to seven, have participants come up with other ways in which teachers actually create additional misbehavior by focusing on currently occurring misbehaviors. Each group should act out its classroom scenario for the entire group. After each group presents, have them discuss ways in which the misbehavior could have been handled differently.

Expectations, Rules, Consequences

Have three large pieces of chart paper posted around the room labeled "Expectations," "Rules," and "Consequences." Have participants work in pairs to brainstorm as many examples as possible for each category. Allow time for each pair to share their lists with the entire group. Ask one member of the group to record each response on the appropriate chart, listing each item only once, but placing a sticker next to an item each time it is repeated. After all responses have been recorded, take time to note which list is the largest and which is the smallest. What does this suggest? Are any "rules" listed that a school can live without or that can be restated as expectations? Are there any "consequences" listed that seem unnecessary or are there other, less punitive options that have not been included as a consequence? Are all items listed as "expectations" truly expectations or did some "rules" sneak onto this list? Remember that the order of emphasis when ranking these three items should be expectations, rules, consequences.

Application

Visit three to five classrooms at different grade levels throughout your school. Take note of any classroom rules, guidelines, expectations, and consequences that are posted in the room. Analyze what you find in light of the information presented in Chapter 3. Are your findings consistent with the principles presented or are most classrooms focusing on rules and consequences for violating rules? Be prepared to share your findings at the next session.

Part Three

Chapter 4: If You Say Something, Mean It

🗝 Key Concepts

♦ When the very best teachers say something, they mean it. They do not depend on a commanding presence or a booming voice to manage their classrooms; rather, students respect their authority because they communicate expectations clearly and follow through consistently.

♦ Great teachers focus on the behavior they expect of their students, not on consequences for misbehavior.

♦ Threatening students is ineffective in creating enduring change. Like shouting or sarcasm, threats may work for a while, but in the long run, the situation gets worse. Effective teachers understand the trade-off between short-term and long-term gains.

♦ All teachers get upset at times. When teachers who are upset blurt out something, it is not likely to be what they would have said had they taken the time to reflect. Therefore, great teachers consciously stop themselves from blurting things out "in the heat of the moment."

♦ Whenever possible, effective teachers wait to deal with misbehavior until they are ready to do so, giving themselves time to calm down and think about the best approach to take.

♦ Maintaining self-control is a critical attribute of great teachers. Great teachers make sure that the expectations and procedures they establish for their class make sense and that they will be able to adhere to them consistently throughout the year.

♦ Classroom management has a lot more to do with *class* than with *management*. One way great teachers exhibit such class is by thinking carefully about—and adhering to—the things they say to students.

1. Why does Whitaker share the story about the football coach? What does it have to do with classroom teachers?

2. Instead of following the adage "Don't smile until Thanksgiving," what does Whitaker suggest?

3. In the section "When You Are Ready," Whitaker shares two anecdotes from his days as a young student with two different teachers. Describe the situations in both classrooms and what they suggest about how effective teachers deal with misbehaving students.

4. Describe three suggestions Whitaker offers regarding calling parents of students who misbehave.

Notes

In this chapter, Whitaker emphasizes the importance of "saying what you mean and meaning what you say." As an example, he tells a story about a football coach who did not follow through on threats he made to his players. Think about a time when a supervisor you worked for (or currently work for) verbally stressed the importance of some rule, procedure, policy, or expectation regarding employee performance but never really followed through or held underperforming employees accountable. Was this supervisor respected? Did all employees consistently adhere to the verbal admonishments over time? Did employee performance and morale improve or decline as a result of these idle threats? How would you have handled that particular situation differently? In what ways does it apply to your classroom and what you say to your students?

_____

_____

_____

_____

_____

_____

_____

_____

_____

_____

_____

_____

_____

_____

_____

_____

_____

Trust Me

Ask participants to move to an open area of the room. Share the following statement with the group: "Students will perform better both academically and behaviorally if they trust their teacher." Ask participants to consider the statement for a minute and then find a partner nearby. Once in pairs, identify one participant as the listener and the other as the speaker. Allow two minutes for participants to speak about the topic of trust and how it impacts relationships in the classroom. Then find a different partner and repeat the process, varying who speaks and who listens. Repeat the process a third time, but this time ask partners to discuss the following seven trust actions:

- ◆ Be there.
- ◆ Show you care.
- ◆ Communicate regularly.
- ◆ Celebrate success.
- ◆ Value diversity and dissent.
- ◆ Address underperformance.
- ◆ Demonstrate personal integrity.

Ask each pair to pick the two they think are most important to establishing trust in their classrooms, explaining why they picked those two and what each looks like in practice. In addition, ask each duo to come up with three more things that teachers can do to establish trust with students (and parents) so that their list of seven becomes ten. Have each pair share their top two actions from their Top 10 list.

Calling All Parents

In the section "From Four to Three" in this chapter, Whitaker offers advice on calling parents. Arrange the group into five teams and have participants discuss this section, noting whether they agree with the advice herein and why. Continue the discussion on calling parents by sharing these five possible guidelines:

1. Call early.
2. Call often.
3. Be honest.
4. Find the good.
5. Listen.

Ask each group to discuss these five guidelines, answering the following questions for each: (1) What exactly does this guideline mean to you or look like in practice? (2) Why would someone suggest this as a guideline for calling parents? (3) To what extent do you agree with the guideline? Next, have each group rank the guidelines in order of importance to them, from most to least important. Finally, call on each group to report their answers by assigning one of the five guidelines to each of the five groups. Have groups first report their ranking of importance for all five guidelines and then share their answers relating to their assigned calling-home guideline.

Notes

In this chapter, the author contrasts the way two different teachers—"The Hammer" and "Mrs. Pro"—reacted to his own misbehavior in their classrooms. Mrs. Pro achieved her desired outcome of improved student behavior by depriving students of the attention they were seeking, focusing on preventing future misbehavior rather than consequences for previous misbehavior, and dealing with individual student misbehavior when she was ready, only after giving herself time to think, calm down, and figure out the best approach. Mrs. Hammer, on the other hand, tried and failed to discipline students through impassioned outbursts and threats.

Upon your return to school, take some time to carefully examine the names of every student on your class roster. Assign students to one of three different categories according to how often they exhibit disruptive behavior in your class: (1) never (2) rarely (3) often. How many students did you put in each category? What have you tried that has worked—and has not—with those students you assigned to Category 3?

Focus on a few students you placed into the third category and try again to reach them in a way that results in improved student performance. The next time these students misbehave, find some time after class or during lunch to speak with them individually. Let them know in a calm, caring, yet firm way that certain behaviors they are exhibiting are negatively impacting themselves, their classmates, and their teacher. Focus on the problematic behaviors rather than the students themselves, explaining why these behaviors are detrimental and cannot be tolerated. Enlist their support in devising a plan for future behavior and ask if they would like you to call their parents so that they, too, can be aware of and support the plan. If they choose not to have their parents notified, say that you will honor that request for now but you will call home if their behavior does not improve, and make sure to follow through on this warning. After meeting with those students who are causing the most disruptions in your class, reflect on whether these private meetings and/or parent phone calls impacted their subsequent behavior. Did it make a difference? Why or why not, in your opinion?

Notes

Part Four

Chapter 5: Prevention versus Revenge

🔑 Key Concepts

- Effective teachers are motivated to prevent misbehavior; ineffective teachers are motivated to punish students who misbehave.

- Effective teachers focus on the future and what they have the ability to influence, rather than on what has already happened.

- Angry students are a problem, not a solution. When a student misbehaves, effective teachers do not want the student to leave the classroom angry; they want the student to behave better in the future.

- All teachers have the same "bag of tricks" available to them in dealing with student behavior.

- The variable is the teacher: great teachers choose wisely from this bag of tricks.

- Students know the difference between right and wrong and generally want the teacher to address inappropriate behavior—in a dignified and respectful manner.

1. Discuss the differences in the ways that effective and ineffective teachers react when a student misbehaves.

2. What do effective teachers need from the principal when they send a student to the office?

3. What are some variables that separate effective classroom managers from ineffective classroom managers?

4. What must teachers do to keep students on their side in supporting appropriate classroom behavior?

5. What are three specific teacher behaviors in every teacher's bag of tricks that great teachers never exhibit?

Notes

Reflect back on a situation (or imagine a situation) in your classroom when, despite your best efforts to clearly establish proactive expectations, you were compelled to refer a misbehaving student to a school administrator. Write about what behavior prompted the office referral and the result of the student's visit to the office. Did the student's behavior change? Did the student come back from the office angry? How did you follow up on the student's misbehavior in the days that followed? In hindsight, would you have changed how you handled the misbehavior? Do you feel that the school administrator should have handled the referral differently?

_____

_____

_____

_____

_____

_____

_____

_____

_____

_____

_____

_____

_____

_____

_____

_____

_____

_____

A Bag of Tricks …

On page 27, the text explains that all teachers have similar options in dealing with student misbehavior, but that great teachers differ from ineffective teachers both in the quantity and quality of "tricks" they employ. Distribute ten slips of paper to each member of the study group. Have each participant list ten different options available to teachers when dealing with student misbehavior, one on each of the ten slips of paper. These should be placed in a bag in the front of the room. Then "pull several tricks from the bag." Take a minute to discuss the relative merits of each option and how many people placed the same or similar option in the bag. End with a discussion of when and how often the study group would choose an office referral as the appropriate action.

The Top Twenty

Have participants read the list of twenty statements related to classroom management below. In small groups, ask them to rank the list in order of importance for establishing an orderly and respectful learning environment. Volunteers can then share their top five and explain their reasoning for choosing these items.

- ◆ I am friendly but firm with my students.
- ◆ I treat each student with kindness and respect.
- ◆ When a student or students act inappropriately, I remain calm and composed.
- ◆ I display enthusiasm and a sense of humor with my students.
- ◆ I give my students a pleasing greeting each day and wish them a pleasant weekend.
- ◆ In order to know what is going on in my classroom, I generally spend my class time on my feet.
- ◆ When I correct student misbehavior, I communicate in a private, positive, and respectful manner.
- ◆ I admit that at times student misbehavior is a result of something that was my fault.
- ◆ I carefully plan each lesson so there is no "dead time."
- ◆ I adjust my daily lesson planning to take into account my students' span of attention.
- ◆ I think through discipline decisions before acting.
- ◆ I make only those discipline decisions that I can enforce.
- ◆ I make discipline decisions after the "heat of the moment" has passed.

- When a student misbehaves in class, I find a way to correct the behavior privately, perhaps by moving near the student and whispering a correction.
- While I take attendance or perform other necessary tasks, often at the outset of each class session, my students are working independently, perhaps on a brief assignment or problem on the overhead or board.
- I establish time-saving routines for collecting papers and distributing materials or supplies.
- I show sincere enthusiasm for the subjects I teach.
- I provide a neat classroom that gives students the idea of orderliness.
- I present a professional appearance in the classroom.
- I insist that my students maintain high standards in their work and behavior. In both areas, my standards are realistic and attainable.

✓ Application

Complete the survey below as a way to self-reflect on your individual discipline practices. Respond to each statement with the following 1–4 ranking. You will be asked at the next session to share what you learned about yourself as a professional educator in completing this survey.

DISCIPLINE PRACTICES SELF-ASSESSMENT

4 = Almost always; 3 = Frequently; 2 = Occasionally; 1 = Almost never

_____ 1. I am friendly but firm with my students.
_____ 2. I treat each student with kindness and respect.
_____ 3. When a student acts inappropriately, I remain calm and composed.
_____ 4. I display enthusiasm and a sense of humor with my students.
_____ 5. During each passing period between classes, I am at the doorway to greet and chat with students.
_____ 6. I interact with all students, not just a few.
_____ 7. I give my students a pleasing greeting each day and wish them a pleasant weekend.
_____ 8. During each passing period between classes, I am at the doorway so I can supervise both the hallway and my classroom.
_____ 9. In order to know what is going on in my classroom, I generally spend my class time on my feet.
_____ 10. I expect students to listen attentively when another student or I am talking.
_____ 11. When I correct student misbehavior, I communicate in a private, positive, respectful manner.

_____ 12. I admit that at times student misbehavior is a result of something that was my fault.

_____ 13. I am able to motivate my students, including the reluctant learner.

_____ 14. I carefully plan each lesson so there is no "dead time."

_____ 15. I provide guided or independent practice during which I move about the room offering individual or small-group assistance.

_____ 16. During each class period, I provide a variety of learning activities. Rarely do I use an entire period for a single activity, as students need a change of pace.

_____ 17. I adjust my daily lesson planning to take into account my students' span of attention.

_____ 18. I think through discipline decisions before acting.

_____ 19. I make only those discipline decisions that I can enforce.

_____ 20. I make discipline decisions after the "heat of the moment" has passed.

_____ 21. When a student misbehaves in class, I find a way to correct the behavior privately, perhaps by moving near the student and whispering a correction.

_____ 22. While I take attendance or perform other necessary tasks, often at the outset of each class session, my students are working independently, perhaps on a brief assignment or problem on the overhead or board.

_____ 23. I establish time-saving routines for collecting papers and distributing materials or supplies.

_____ 24. My directions for a learning activity are brief and concise.

_____ 25. I give directions one step at a time. I avoid long and detailed directions.

_____ 26. I show sincere enthusiasm for the subjects I teach.

_____ 27. I provide a neat classroom that gives students the idea of orderliness.

_____ 28. I present a professional appearance in the classroom.

_____ 29. I insist that my students maintain high standards in their work and behavior. In both areas, my standards are realistic and attainable.

_____ 30. Because there is no "best" teaching method, my methods and learning activities are many and varied.

_____ 31. My homework assignments have a purpose, are instructional, and are regulated as to the time it will take a student to complete them.

_____ 32. I make my classroom attractive by designing effective bulletin boards related to the topics that the class is studying at the time.

_____ 33. During each class session, I summarize, or have students summarize, the day's learning.

_____ 34. I use pretests or other procedures to ascertain what students already know.

Part Five

Chapter 6: High Expectations— for Whom?
Chapter 7: Who Is the Variable?

🔑 Key Concepts

- All teachers, even ineffective teachers, have high expectations for students. The difference is that great teachers also have very high expectations of themselves.

- When students are not focused and engaged in the classroom, great teachers ask themselves what *they* can do differently to improve student engagement.

- The main variable in any classroom is not the students, but the teacher.

- Effective teachers always strive to improve and they focus on something they can control: their own behavior.

- Just as successful students and parents accept responsibility, the most effective teachers accept responsibility for their performance in the classroom.

? Discussion Questions

1. What is the variable in terms of teacher expectations?

2. Do you feel that it is accurate to state that most principals can predict which teachers will send the most students to the office each year? Explain.

3. How do ineffective teachers and effective teachers react when their students do poorly on an assessment? Is there a difference? If so, why?

4. Why do successful teachers insist on focusing on their own behavior rather than the behavior of others (parents, administrators, students, etc.)?

5. How are effective teachers similar to the effective business managers that the text mentions?

Notes

Throughout these two chapters, the book stresses the belief that teachers should take responsibility for what happens in their classrooms. It is suggested that if teachers all look in the mirror each time they ask, "Who is the variable?" they will have made great strides toward school improvement. Take a few moments to write about your thoughts on this concept. Next, reflect in writing about the role of student, parent, and teacher responsibility in ensuring academic success for each student you teach.

_____

_____

_____

_____

_____

_____

_____

_____

_____

_____

_____

_____

_____

_____

_____

_____

_____

_____

_____

_____

_____

_____

Expectations—For Everyone

In the journal entry for Part 2 of this *Study Guide*, participants were asked to list three to five expectations for student behavior that they deemed of vital importance. Working in groups of two to five, have them reexamine the issue of expectations from the perspectives of students and parents. What are a few expectations for which all stakeholders should hold all teachers accountable? Ask participants to list these as "We will" statements, such as "We (as teachers) will treat all members of our school community with dignity and respect." Have them write five "We will" statements to which they would expect teachers to adhere. Then have them share their lists, recording answers on the board, overhead, chart paper, or computer screen. After each group has shared, ask participants to decide which of these statements are the five most important.

Mission, Vision, Values

Provide a number of mission, vision, and value statements from schools, businesses, and other organizations. Discuss, as a group, the definitions and differences among these three commonly used terms (*mission*: what your purpose is; *vision*: what you hope to become; *values*: what commitments you are willing to adopt in order to make your vision a reality). Divide participants into three groups, a "mission" group, a "vision" group, and a "values" group. Each group will create a mission, vision, or value statement for a great teacher. After sharing these group statements, ask participants to create their own individual mission, vision, and value statements for themselves as a classroom teacher.

Notes

Application

Upon returning to your classroom, engage in instructional self-reflection for a full week. At the end of each day, identify one teaching activity that did not go as well as you had envisioned. List three adjustments you will try the next time you teach that lesson in order to make the lesson successful for the learners. Looking at yourself should always be the first reflective step of a great teacher. In the next session, you will have the opportunity to discuss your progress during this instructional reflection activity.

Notes

Part Six

Chapter 8: Focus on Students First

🔑 Key Concepts

- Although it is easy to *say* "Put students first" and "Make every decision based on what is best for students," not all teachers manage to *do* so, yet some do so more consistently than others.

- "Superstar" teachers have a broad vision, taking into account the whole school setting in everything they do and every decision they make. They consider how their actions impact the entire school.

- "Backbone" teachers—although caring and solid educators—typically have a vision that is limited to their own classroom walls.

- The least effective teachers in the school typically have a more narrow vision still—a vision only as wide as the mirror on the wall. They make decisions and respond to change by asking, "What does this mean for me?"

- Great teachers resist the temptation to socialize when they should be supervising. They know the value of interacting with other teachers—and so they treat their colleagues as the *second* most important group of people in the school.

- Teaching is hard. Complaining about school-related problems may feel good momentarily, but it does not make the job of teaching any easier. In fact, when negativity spreads—as it easily can—it actually makes the job much harder. Great teachers avoid falling into the trap of complaining.

- One of the best things about being a teacher is that teaching matters—especially to students. What teachers do makes a profound impact in the lives of students. Great teachers, therefore, make it a point to put students first every day, which helps them make a difference all the way to the end of the school year.

1. What are the three different types of teachers at any school? What are their corresponding visions?

2. Describe how the three different teachers react to the Tuesday morning announcement of the principal at "Riverdale High" and the same situation with two weeks' advance notice. Whom was the best teacher most concerned about in the scenarios?

3. Name two ways that complaining about your job as a teacher is analogous to the well-known song "Hotel California" by the Eagles. What is Whitaker's point in sharing this analogy?

4. How can focusing on "students first" help you maintain a positive attitude about your role as a teacher?

5. Why does Whitaker include a reference to the musical *The King and I*? Why does he say that Anna is a "great teacher"? How does this reference relate to great teachers who focus on students first?

Notes

Teaching is a very demanding profession and teachers are often faced with stressful, even unfair situations. Yet, as Whitaker suggests, although complaining about such situations can be tempting, in the long run it only serves to make the job even more difficult. Anyone who has worked in education—or, for that matter, in any profession—for even a few years has probably worked with colleagues who were chronic complainers. Think of three teachers at your school whom you perceive as chronic complainers. Next, think of three teachers at your school whom you have rarely, if ever, heard complain. Is there a difference between these two groups in terms of their job performance? Do you enjoy being in the company of one group more than the other? Which group seems to be having the most fun at school? Is there a difference in the attendance pattern between the two groups? Do the chronic complainers ever subtly encourage you and others to join in the "gripe fest"? Why is it vitally important that educators remain positive about their jobs and their profession?

_____

_____

_____

_____

_____

_____

_____

_____

_____

_____

_____

_____

_____

"Students First" Teachers

Have participants identify the characteristics of "students first" teachers and teaching by completing the following activity (have participants begin in table groups):

♦ Step 1: Have each person take four index cards from the table stack, writing one characteristic of "students first" teachers or teaching on each card.

♦ Step 2: Collect and shuffle the cards and deal out three to each participant. Arrange the remaining cards on a table.

♦ Step 3: Ask participants to silently arrange their three cards from "most important" to "least important."

♦ Step 4: Each participant may pick up better replacement cards from the table, but must discard a card for each one picked up.

♦ Step 5: Participants may now talk and swap cards with one another. Everyone must exchange at least one card.

♦ Step 6: Participants should compare cards and form teams of three to six people who hold similar cards.

♦ Step 7: Have teams reduce the number of cards to no more than three per team.

♦ Step 9: Have each team use flip-chart paper and markers to prepare a graphic poster that reflects the three final cards. This poster should not include any text. (Allow six to eight minutes.)

♦ Step 9: Have each team, in turn, display their poster silently. Members of other teams will guess aloud the characteristics of "students first" teachers and teaching depicted in the poster. After fifteen seconds, ask members of the display team to read the characteristics listed on their cards.

Believing in Students

Write each of the following ten statements on an index card (if there are more than twenty participants, create additional statements that probe teacher beliefs about "students first" teachers and teaching):

1. Most students in our school are capable of mastering grade-level learning objectives.
2. Students at our school consistently behave appropriately.
3. Teachers at our school believe that most students are able to master core content standards.

4. My expectations for students influence how well they will perform academically.

5. My expectations for students will influence how well they behave at school.

6. Nearly all of my students will be at or above grade level by the end of the school year.

7. Some of our students are destined to fail classes or fail to meet learning expectations.

8. Teachers at our school consistently base their decisions on what is best for students.

9. Teachers should treat all students with dignity and respect at all times.

10. Complaining about students or their parents is never appropriate.

Ask participants to stand in two concentric circles, facing a partner. Give each participant in the inner circle one of the index cards. Have them ask their partners in the outer circle to discuss their level of agreement with the statement on the index card, based on a scale of 1 ("strongly disagree") to 4 ("strongly agree").

After two minutes, have partners in the outer or inner circle rotate to the next partner. (The group leader may call rotation numbers: "Rotate three ahead.") Continue for three or four rotations.

Collect the index cards and give them to the participants in the outer circle. Repeat the process three or four more times with the roles of speaker and listener reversed. Debrief the process by asking participants to share their thoughts on how these statements may or may not define "students first" teachers and teaching.

Notes

✓ Application

As the author notes at the start of this chapter, it is quite easy to say "Make every decision based on what is best for students"; very few, if any, educators would disagree with this statement. Yet in all schools adults make some decisions based on something other than that standard, such as basing the decision on what is easiest, or what is least expensive, or what will result in the least amount of conflict, or what was done in similar situations in the past, or what is best for teachers, administrators, and parents.

Between now and the next study group meeting, keep a list of decisions that have to be made at your school and in your classroom. For each decision, consciously ask yourself, "What would be the best option for the students I teach?" In addition, pose the same question about the following three scenarios, which occur in almost all classrooms in nearly all schools. Scenario 1: A student in your class fails to turn in a major assignment on the due date. Scenario 2: A student misbehaves in your class almost every day, disrupting the learning environment. Scenario 3: A student in your class is often absent and has missed your class four days out of the past ten. For each scenario, how would you respond if your sole standard was to do what was best for the individual student in question? Would your decision be different if you were focusing on what was best for all students in your class? Why or why not? Be prepared to share your answers at the next study group meeting.

Notes

Part Seven

Chapter 9: Ten Days Out of Ten

🔑 Key Concepts

- Great teachers create a positive atmosphere each day in their classrooms despite inevitable negatives such as irate parents, troubled students, and limited resources.

- Effective teachers treat everyone with dignity and respect ten days out of ten. They may not like all their students, but they *act* as if they do.

- Students may remember the times teachers treat them well, but they will *always* remember when they were treated disrespectfully or unfairly—even if it is only one time.

- Effective teachers understand the power of praise and look for opportunities to find people doing things right.

- To be effective, praise must be *authentic, specific, immediate, clean,* and *private.*

- Focusing on all the positive things in their classrooms and schools gives teachers the drive and energy to get through the less positive times.

- Effective teachers know that one of a teacher's most important tasks is to model appropriate behavior. Great teachers, therefore, model the behavior of treating all people with dignity and respect all the time.

1. Why must great teachers always act as if they like all their students?

2. Define the five necessary attributes of effective praise: authentic, specific, immediate, clean, and private. Explain why each is important and provide an example. Which of the five characteristics is often most challenging for educators? Why? Who determines how much you praise someone? Who feels better each time you do?

3. What are three myths often used in rationalizing why teachers do not praise more often? Offer an argument debunking each myth.

Notes

All of us can recall an occasion in our professional lives when someone in a leadership role treated us inappropriately. Think of such a time in your own adult life when this happened. Is it, indeed, etched into your memory? Can you recall a similar situation from your own school career in grades K–12 when a teacher made a cutting remark or acted rudely toward you? Describe a situation from that time and how it made you feel. Did it change your opinion of that particular teacher?

Group Activities

The Power of Praise

On page 51, the text details Bissell's five traits that make praise work, noting that, to be effective, praise must be *authentic, specific, immediate, clean, and private*. After organizing the participants into several groups, have one group role-play a classroom scene in which a "teacher" praises "students" while clearly demonstrating authenticity, specificity, immediacy, cleanliness, and privacy. Ask other groups to portray a teacher using praise, but omitting one of the five requirements of effective praise. Have other participants identify which of the five requirements was violated. After the role-plays, have the entire group discuss what they think is the most important of the five characteristics of effective praise.

Our Cup Runneth Over!

In this chapter, the text emphasizes that focusing on the positive elements of classrooms and schools will give teachers more drive and energy as they face their daily work. Divide participants into groups of three to five. Give each group a piece of chart paper with a large cup or glass drawn on it and a package of self-stick notes. Have participants "fill" their cup with examples of positive, productive things happening in their classrooms and schools by writing brief descriptions on the sticky notes and placing them inside the cup. Allow time for individuals to share within their groups. Then ask each group to choose and share their top five positive ideas with the entire group. Post these charts for all to read and discuss.

 Application

On page 55, the text notes that one reason teachers give for not praising more is lack of time. Make the time during the next five school days to praise at least five different students and five different colleagues. For the students, the praise should take the form of a phone call to parents praising a specific behavior or accomplishment or a postcard or handwritten note sent home in the mail. For colleagues, send a positive note via the teacher's mailbox. At the next session, report your reaction to this activity, as well as the reactions of the people you praised.

Part Eight

Chapter 10: Be the Filter

🔑 Key Concepts

♦ The teacher is the filter who models appropriate behavior in the classroom. If the model teachers establish is positive and professional, students will match it; if the teacher's attitude is negative and confrontational, students will respond in kind.

♦ The teacher's goal in class should be to make students more excited about learning tomorrow than they were today.

♦ Great teachers realize that teaching is a demanding job, yet they focus on its rewards and challenges in a positive way rather than complaining.

♦ The best teachers are professionals who keep personal issues private and also keep school issues in their place. They do not involve students in inappropriate topics.

♦ Teachers' own perceptions of their school and their students impact the reality of their school and students. Teachers have the power to decide the tone of their school and how they view their students.

1. In what ways do teachers serve as "filters" at the schools in which they teach?

2. In what ways can choosing not to share information with colleagues create a more productive environment?

3. Explain the statement "When the teacher sneezes, the whole class catches a cold."

4. How can great teachers counteract colleagues prone to complaining about teaching, students, and administration?

5. Examine the often heard refrain "This is the worst group of kids we've ever had." Why do some teachers say this? What are the effects of saying this? How can teachers change this mentality?

Notes

Take a moment to consider the negative comments you might hear during the course of a week from students, other teachers, administrators, and parents. Recall from the text that by constantly filtering out such negatives that do not matter and instead maintaining a positive attitude, teachers can create a much more successful school environment. Write about typical negatives you might hear from any of these groups of school stakeholders and how you could, in the future, filter out such comments and even alter these perceptions by offering a different perception.

_____

_____

_____

_____

_____

_____

_____

_____

_____

_____

_____

_____

_____

_____

_____

_____

_____

_____

Circle of Friends

Arrange participants into two concentric circles with partners facing each other. Have the people in the inner circle relate an example of negativity at their school. The person in the outer circle should listen carefully and offer suggestions for dealing with this difficult and negative person and/or situation. After five minutes, have the inner circle rotate three places to the right. Repeat the activity, this time asking the people in the outer circle to share their negative scenarios. Repeat once or twice. Then, have the entire group share what was learned. Did most participants share similar stories? What were the most useful strategies for dealing with negative people and situations?

Filtering Out the Insignificant

Post this sentence on the board or chart paper:

> FINISHED FILES ARE THE RESULTS OF YEARS
> OF SCIENTIFIC STUDY COMBINED WITH
> THE EXPERIENCE OF YEARS.

Ask participants to count aloud the *F*s in the sentence and count them only once. Participants should not try to look back and count them a second time.

How many *F*s did everyone count? Many people count three or four, but there are actually six. The reason that nearly everyone undercounts is that the mind automatically *filters out* the *F*s in the word *of*, which is included three times in the sentence. Have participants pair up with a partner and discuss how this activity is analogous to filtering out the negatives at school. Like the word *of*, negativity is rampant; if teachers focus on every *of* or every negative thing they hear, they will miss the big picture—the meaning of what it is they are involved in, whether that is reading or teaching.

Notes

✓ Application

Make a conscious decision, upon your return to your school, to filter out negative situations that inevitably face you, whether they come from inside or outside the school. Respond cheerfully to any colleague who asks you how you are doing. Politely dismiss any negative comments made by your teaching peers. Brag about your students each day to anyone who will listen. Tell your students at the end of each day that you can't wait to return to school the following day because you are so excited about what they will be learning tomorrow. After doing this for several consecutive days, record in your study guide any changes you have noticed in your own perspective or those of others, including students you teach and your colleagues.

Notes

Part Nine

Chapter 11: Don't Need to Repair– Always Do Repair

🔑 Key Concepts

- Effective educators know that a relationship, once damaged, may never be the same.

- The best teachers seldom need to do any emotional repairing in their classrooms, but they are continually working to repair, just in case.

- Great teachers learn to say "I am so sorry that happened" as a way to defuse tense situations and repair relationships.

- Great teachers practice behaviors for repairing a situation; they also teach students behaviors for repairing, rather than escalating, a negative situation.

- Great teachers work hard to keep their relationships in good repair—to avoid personal hurt and to repair any possible damage—and other people notice this effort.

1. What is likely to happen in the classroom when educators become impatient and unprofessional?

2. What are several ways that an effective teacher consistently works to repair relationships?

3. Why might an effective teacher apologize to a class the day after a less-than-ideal lesson? Why do less effective teachers fail to recognize the need to repair and why do they seldom work to repair? How can teachers work to change this pattern of behavior?

4. Why is the simple act of saying "I am sorry that happened" such a powerful tool?

5. How do effective teachers take advantage of teachable moments to help students build the skill of repairing?

Notes

Imagine (or draw on your own experience) a situation in which parents are visibly upset with you about an incident at school involving their son or daughter (a bad grade, a demeaning comment allegedly made about the child, a punishment that they consider unjust, etc.). Write about this situation and how it would play out if your immediate response was "I am sorry that happened." Write out a script of responses and follow-up replies in such a situation. Remember: you are not saying that the incident was your fault or accepting blame; rather, you are simply starting off by expressing your sorrow that it happened.

_____

_____

_____

_____

_____

_____

_____

_____

_____

_____

_____

_____

_____

_____

_____

_____

_____

_____

Group Activities

The Builder

Have the group read the poem "The Builder" below. In pairs, have participants discuss how the themes of the poem relate to the themes of Chapter 11 (e.g., "repairing" and "building"). Have participants try their hand at rewriting the poem for the role of a teacher, creating ten rhyming couplets, but keeping the final couplet in its current form. Remind participants that, as teachers, they have tremendous influence to build up or tear down their students and that they must commit to serving as a builder and repairer, rather than one who tears down. Have participants share their newly created poems with the whole group.

The Builder

I saw a group of men tearing a building down,
A group of men in my hometown.

With a heave and a ho and a mighty yell,
They swung a beam and a side wall fell.

And I said to the foreman, "Are those men skilled?
The type you'd hire if you wanted to build?"

He laughed and replied, "Why, no indeed."
He said, "Common labor is all I need.

Why, I can tear down in a day or two
What it takes a builder ten years to do."

And I thought to myself as I walked away,
Which of these roles am I going to play?

(Author Unknown)

A Restorative Approach

Whitaker's book advises educators to teach misbehaving students to behave in a way that "restores" them in the eyes of the offended party. In a traditional approach to discipline, the focus is on (1) What happened? (2) Who's to blame? (3) What's the punishment? On the other hand, a restorative approach asks (1) What happened? (2) Who has been affected and how? (3) How can we put it right? (4) What have we learned so that we can make different choices next time?

Divide the participants into four groups. Give each group a card containing a common school scenario in which someone is adversely affected—for example, a student consistently talks out in class, a student responds disrespectfully to a teacher, a student refuses to complete an assignment, a student uses inappropriate or threatening language toward a classmate. Have each group analyze their assigned scenario and plan out two courses of action, one based on the traditional approach and the other on the restorative approach. Have the groups post their two plans on chart paper and present to the entire group. Discuss the benefits and disadvantages of the two approaches while focusing on the goals of restoration and repairing.

Application

On page 69 of the text, the author describes getting stopped for speeding by the highway patrol and notes that his goal was to avoid getting a ticket. Ask your students if they have ever been in a situation in which they were about to get in big trouble, but managed to minimize the consequence. Relate the story the author tells, tweaking it as appropriate to fit the situation at hand. Teach the students behavior strategies for staying out of trouble—or at least minimizing the severity of the consequence by reacting appropriately—as you share this story. Emphasize the importance of apologizing and treating the offended party with dignity and respect. Observe the students' reactions and note whether any student employs these behaviors in ensuing days. This activity will be discussed in the next session.

Notes

Part Ten

Chapter 12: The Ability to Ignore

🗝 Key Concepts

- Great teachers are aware of almost everything that happens in their classroom, and they know which situations demand immediate attention and which can wait for a more teachable moment.

- Effective teachers model self-control; their classroom management is grounded in their ability to manage their own behavior.

- Great teachers do not automatically react every time a student steps a little out of line.

- The great teacher has the ability to pay attention to students, to recognize and praise their achievements, and to overlook minor errors.

- High achievers put so much of themselves into what they do that any criticism, no matter how minor, can become a personal affront. This is true of both high-achieving students and high-achieving teachers.

? Discussion Questions

1. Why do great teachers ignore certain behaviors?

2. Why do most students misbehave?

3. What is the likely outcome when teachers continually nitpick about a student's behavior? About a student's academic performance?

4. In what ways does the information in this chapter relate specifically to high achievers?

5. How do great teachers balance the contradictory themes of ignoring certain behaviors and paying attention to those students who crave it?

Notes

Journal Prompt

The author notes the advice of a friend who is a police officer: "You can look for trouble or you can look away." Similarly, William James famously theorized, "The art of being wise is knowing what to overlook." Take a moment to write your reactions to these two quotes as they relate to the classroom setting. What behaviors that often occur in the classroom should teachers regularly overlook? When should they go with the flow and when should they stop and take a stand? How do they determine which disturbances are trivial and should be ignored and which should be responded to? How can they respond without escalating the situation?

_____

_____

_____

_____

_____

_____

_____

_____

_____

_____

_____

_____

_____

_____

_____

_____

_____

_____

_____

_____

Ignore and Intervene Pointers

Divide participants into small groups of three or four. Have them review the following two lists suggesting when to ignore certain behaviors and when to intervene. After reading and discussing both lists thoroughly, have participants read the ten behaviors in the table below and determine which of these behaviors they would ignore and which require intervention. Each group will report back to the whole group. Compare and contrast group responses.

Pointers for when to ignore behavior:

- when the inappropriate behavior is unintentional or not likely to recur
- when the goal of the misbehavior is to gain the teacher's attention
- when you want the behavior to decrease
- when there is nothing you can do

Pointers for when to intervene:

- when the misbehavior might cause physical danger or harm to yourself, the student, or others
- when a student disrupts the classroom
- when the misbehavior violates classroom rules or school policy
- when the misbehavior interferes with learning
- when the inappropriate behavior might spread to other students

Behavior	Ignore	Intervene
A student is tapping a pencil on his desktop.		
A student repeatedly taps his pencil on his desk, disturbing others in the classroom.		
Every time a particular student enters the classroom, she intentionally kicks the trash can, causing the rest of the class to laugh.		
A student enters the classroom and accidentally kicks the trash can.		
A student gets out of his seat to sharpen his pencil.		
A student blurts out the response to a question without raising her hand.		
A student is yanking on the ponytail of a student seated in front of him.		

Behavior	Ignore	Intervene
A student calls another student a "fatso" while lining up for lunch.		
During independent reading time, a student is silently reading the assignment but has a Power Ranger displayed on her desk.		
A student is writing on the surface of his desk with a permanent marker.		

Acting It Out

Divide participants into groups of five to seven and have each group prepare a skit involving a classroom situation. In the skits, each group should include three student misbehaviors, two of which they think an effective teacher would ignore and one that they feel an effective teacher would deal with. In each presentation, have the "teacher" deal with all three behaviors. After each skit, have the other groups decide which of the three behaviors was the one that merited the teacher's response.

 Application

Arrange for someone at your school to videotape you teaching for fifteen to thirty minutes. Review the tape and analyze your teaching behaviors, paying particular attention to the way in which you responded—or chose not to respond—to student misbehavior. Make a written record of the strengths and weaknesses you observed in your ability to maintain positive classroom management. Make a second videotape in several weeks and compare your findings.

Notes

Part Eleven

Chapter 13: Random or Plandom?
Chapter 14: Base Every Decision on the Best People

🔑 Key Concepts

- Great teachers have a plan and purpose for everything they do. They reflect on what did and did not work and adjust accordingly.

- Great teachers take responsibility for what happens and plan for success. Less effective teachers allow classroom events to happen randomly and then blame others when things do not work out well.

- Great teachers expect and plan for appropriate student behavior by ensuring that certain students do—or do not—work together. Great teachers proactively anticipate student misbehavior and plan to eliminate it before it occurs.

- Great teachers intentionally arrange, rearrange, alter, and adjust the structures that frame their teaching. Their classroom setup, their instructional approaches, and their time management are all carefully planned to promote an optimal learning environment.

- Great teachers do not try to prove who is in charge of their classrooms; everyone already knows.

- Great teachers make decisions based on three simple factors: (1) What is the purpose? (2) Will this actually accomplish the purpose? (3) What will the best people think?

- Great teachers always treat students as if the students' parents were in the room. They deal with students who disrupt learning, but they do it respectfully.

- Great teachers do not "teach to the middle." Instead, they ensure that every student is engaged. They ask, "What will my best students think?" and teach all students accordingly, considering the best, most well-rounded students at the forefront when making decisions.

❓ Discussion Questions

1. What is the most important idea communicated in these two chapters? How would you implement this idea in your classroom? Are there any ideas in these chapters with which you disagree?

2. How do great teachers respond when classroom events do not occur as planned?

3. How do great teachers differ from ineffective teachers in preventing and dealing with student misbehavior?

4. What are three simple guidelines great teachers use in making decisions?

5. Why is it important to focus on the purpose, and not the reason, when making decisions?

6. Why should teachers avoid "teaching to the middle" of the class?

7. How do great teachers change the dynamics of a classroom without engaging in power struggles?

8. What do the best students expect teachers to do about student misbehavior?

Think of a teacher you know—or who taught you—in whose classroom events always seemed carefully planned. Was this teacher effective? Describe a teacher you had or know who always considers her very best students when making decisions regarding teaching and learning.

_____

_____

_____

_____

_____

_____

_____

_____

_____

_____

_____

_____

_____

_____

_____

_____

_____

_____

_____

_____

_____

Group Activities

Graffiti on the Walls

On page 87 of the text, there is reference to a school whose principal ordered the bathroom stall doors removed in order to prevent students from writing on the stalls. Divide the participants into small groups and have them discuss the following questions: What was the purpose of this decision? Will this decision accomplish the goal? How will the best students feel as a result of this decision? What other steps could the principal have taken to eradicate the problem of graffiti on the bathroom walls, keeping in mind whether the proposed action will accomplish the purpose and what the best students will think of the plan? Have each group share their ideas with the whole group.

More Math Homework

Ask participants to imagine that they are teaching at a school in which recent standardized assessments suggest that students are performing well below average in math. As a result, the principal has directed all teachers to assign more math homework daily. Accepting the assumption that all teachers must comply with this directive, ask participants to think about the best way to move forward, keeping in mind the purpose of raising test scores, whether or not more homework will accomplish the purpose, and what the best students will think. Next, have participants pair up with a colleague and share what they decided with each other. Have several pairs volunteer their insights to the entire study group.

Random/Plandom

On page 79 of the text, the book discusses at length the "structural" things that teachers can do to plan for success, such as grouping students together, using seating charts, and maintaining proximity control. Divide participants into groups of three to five and have them create a list of ten specific classroom occurrences that may result from a teacher's failure to plan carefully for a successful lesson, situation, or behavior. Then have participants create a second list of ten classroom occurrences that may result when a teacher carefully plans for successful learning and behavior. Place these brainstorming lists on two pieces of chart paper labeled "Random" and "Plandom," respectively. Have each group post their chart on a wall. One person from each group should present their lists to the whole group.

✓ Application

Choose one concept from these two chapters that you find laudable as well as transferable to your own classroom and incorporate it into your daily professional life. Record your progress toward this goal in your journal over the next few weeks, noting specific occasions when you utilized this concept in your classroom. Arrange through your principal and a colleague you respect to observe in that colleague's room for twenty minutes one day. Identify ways in which this colleague practices the tenets of "plandomness" over "randomness." Write these down and share them at the next session.

Notes

Part Twelve

Chapter 15: In Every Situation, Ask Who Is Most Comfortable and Who Is Least Comfortable

🔑 Key Concepts

- Great teachers avoid lecturing the entire class about rules and never punish the entire class because of a few students' misbehavior.

- Great teachers know that the best students will feel uncomfortable if a teacher yells or uses cutting remarks, even when directed at a student who is misbehaving.

- Effective educators attempt to make people who do the right thing feel comfortable. They reinforce such people and such behaviors.

- Effective teachers never place the very best students in the position of being uncomfortable for doing the right thing.

- Great teachers treat everyone as if they are good and continually ask themselves who is most comfortable and who is least comfortable with each decision they make.

1. What is the one internal standard that supports effective practices when making decisions that follow no clearly stated rule?

2. What is the flawed thinking in sending home a note to all parents about a policy being broken by only a handful of those same parents?

3. What happens when people are made to feel uncomfortable? What happens when people feel comfortable?

4. Why is it unwise for teachers to have students "trade and grade" each other's schoolwork?

5. How should teachers apply the "most comfortable/least comfortable" ground rule when dealing with belligerent parents?

Notes

On page 94, Whitaker refers to a "Pay for Performance" program in use at a university and the varying reactions to the program based on a survey of all participants. The author suggests, instead, that the perspective of the entire faculty should not be the decisive factor. Instead, he advises surveying only the top one-third of the faculty to solicit their level of comfort with the program. Explain why he suggests this and how it relates to the chapter title. Think of a situation at your own school when you have felt uncomfortable with an action that was taken, in your opinion, as a response to poor performance on the part of mediocre teachers. How did this make you feel? What could have been done differently to address the problem?

Dear Parents ...

On page 90 of the text, the author shares a memo sent home to all parents regarding picking up their children on time after school. He also includes an alternative letter that is just as effective as a reminder to the parents who are the problem while reinforcing the good behavior of the majority of the parents. In groups of three to five, have participants brainstorm other issues that result in a letter home to parents (attendance, signing and returning paperwork, tardiness, making up work, discipline, sending children with appropriate materials, etc.). Each group should choose one topic and write two versions of a letter to parents addressing the issue. The first letter should be written following the traditional approach, targeting all parents equally. The second letter should be written in the alternative style, attempting to make the parents who act correctly feel comfortable, while perhaps making the others feel slightly uncomfortable in the hopes they will change the behavior.

Dealing with Difficult Parents

On page 93, Whitaker discusses the fact that when a belligerent parent engages a teacher in an argument, it is often the teacher, not the parent, who feels uncomfortable. Divide the study group into five sections and assign one of the following tips for dealing with difficult parents to each group:

1. Approach difficult situations and difficult parents with an attitude of respect and a willingness to listen. Remember that you and the parents have one thing in common: the desire for their children to succeed.
2. Address specific complaints with ideas about what you and the parents can do together to find a solution.
3. Exercise empathy—always take some time to walk in the parents' shoes and try to gain an understanding of their perspective.
4. Express an attitude that is pleasant, not defensive or negative.
5. Keep tense conversations focused on the student by saying, "I care about your child." This will not only soften a difficult parent's attitude, but also prevent the teacher from feeling persecuted.

Each group should examine their assigned tip and report back to the large group their thoughts on the suggestion. Have each group brainstorm situations in which they could employ the technique and role-play a situation in which they practice the suggestion. After each group has presented their assigned tip, ask volunteers to share other effective ways of dealing with difficult parents. Remind participants that great teachers do not fall into the trap of arguing with parents or responding defensively.

 **Application**

Upon returning to your school, examine any student handbooks, parent communications, course outlines, syllabi, and codes of conducts you can locate. Apply the *Who is most comfortable and who is least comfortable in this situation?* standard to each document. Find examples of language that might make your best stakeholders feel uncomfortable while doing little to address those who might truly need to understand the directives and change their behavior. Bring any examples you find to the next study session.

Notes

Part Thirteen

Chapter 16: Put Yourself in Their Position

🔑 Key Concepts

- Even when a group of students look pretty much the same, great teachers know that every student has unique strengths and needs, ideas and emotions, troubles and joys. Great teachers work effectively with all students by remembering to put themselves in their students' shoes periodically.

- Schools today serve students of all backgrounds with all manner of special needs and circumstances. Effective teachers do not shy away from these challenges; instead, they embrace them. Great teachers have the ability to see the world the way their individual students do.

- All teachers know about the part of their job that involves teaching their content area. Great teachers give equal weight to the part of teaching that involves teaching "people skills." They think of this task as shaping the good neighbors, responsible citizens, and capable parents of tomorrow.

- Effective teachers have a keen sense of self-awareness. They know their strengths and weaknesses and consistently try to build on the former and improve on the latter.

- Great teachers take time to focus on their physical self. They realize that taking care of themselves helps them "get out of their own way" so they can see the other person's position.

- Great teachers are lifelong learners who regularly attempt to learn something new. Becoming "students" again allows great teachers to put themselves in their students' shoes.

- Great teachers realize they are not perfect and are constantly trying to improve their skills as a teacher. One way they do so is by inviting other teachers to observe them while they are teaching and by soliciting tips for connecting with students.

1. In what ways is every classroom in America heterogeneous regardless of how similar students may look on the surface?

2. Whitaker suggests that many teachers today were "teacher pleasers" when they were students. What must such teachers realize when they move from the role of student to teacher?

3. In what ways do great teachers model what they expect from their students? What do ineffective teachers do instead?

4. Why is it so important for teachers to accurately perceive how they come across to others—in particular, their students?

5. Do you agree with what Whitaker suggests about staying physically active, eating properly, and being a lifelong learner? Why or why not? How does each of these habits impact your effectiveness in the classroom?

6. Why does Whitaker suggest that teachers ask a superstar teacher in the building to observe them while teaching?

Notes

✏ Journal Prompt

Whitaker notes that "in one way or another, every classroom is heterogeneous." Think about the students you teach (or have taught) in the course of a school day. How many are male? Female? How many live with both their mother and father? How many are identified as having a learning, behavior, or physical disability? How many are students for whom English is not their primary language? Are some living in poverty? Are any experiencing traumatic situations in their personal lives? How many different religions, races, and cultures are represented by the students you teach? In what ways are your personal characteristics similar or different from those of the majority of your students? Do you have ways to learn more about the individual circumstances of each of your students outside of school? If so, can you better relate to and work with these students once you know them better? What steps can you take to intentionally put yourself in your students' shoes from time to time?

_____

_____

_____

_____

_____

_____

_____

_____

_____

_____

_____

_____

_____

_____

_____

The Student Perspective

Ask participants to put themselves into their students' minds, looking out through their eyes: how would the teachers and their classrooms come across? Suggest that the best way to find out how they and their classrooms come across is to actually ask their students.

Have individual participants jot down several questions they might ask their students that would provide them with meaningful feedback. Next, group participants into teams of two or three (grouping by content area or grade level, if possible). Have group members share the questions they devised and why they chose those questions. Then, allow fifteen minutes for each group to compile a list of fifteen to twenty questions that would be appropriate to ask their students in order to gain student insights into their teaching, their content, and their classrooms.

For example, it would certainly be appropriate to ask, "What was your favorite unit this semester?" but also ask, "Why?" Specific details are much more useful. Questions could involve everything from the teacher's classroom management style, to the seating arrangement, to the assignments and assessments students are asked to complete.

Have participants take this survey back to their classrooms and have their students complete them—anonymously. Students will often give teachers great ideas and very honest feedback. Study group leaders should also consider having participants create a second survey to be completed by the parents of students they teach. Participants may want to use Survey Monkey or another online tool to administer both surveys.

Understanding Student Behaviors and Responding Effectively

Place four pieces of chart paper around the room with one of the following headings on each:

- ◆ Disengaged Student
- ◆ Distracting Student
- ◆ Attention-Getting Student
- ◆ Disrespectful Student

Arrange participants into four groups and ask each group to move to one of the four chart papers. Each team should write on the chart paper a one-sentence "definition" of the student type to which they have been assigned. Next, ask them to write answers to the following questions: What behaviors might such students demonstrate? What work habits might such students have? Why do you think these students act in these ways?

After each group has completed the above directions, ask one person from each group to share with the whole group the definitions, characteristics, and motivations of students in their category. After all groups have presented, distribute sticky notes to each participant. Allow each group to travel to each of the four posters and list as many ideas as they can for dealing effectively with the student type described on the chart paper, listing one idea per sticky note. After five minutes, have them rotate to the next poster and continue until all groups have traveled to all four posters.

To debrief the activity, have participants move back to their original poster, reviewing all suggestions and deciding on the three they think are most helpful. Ask each group to share the three suggestions they found most useful with the whole group.

✓ Application

In this chapter, the author stresses the importance of practicing empathy, the ability to understand or imagine things from another person's perspective—in this case, the perspectives of individual students. He closes the chapter by exhorting teachers to become the type of teacher they would want their own children to have. One way to achieve this lofty aim is to continuously find ways to connect with the students they teach.

Upon returning to your school, take up Whitaker's challenge in the final paragraph by asking the best teacher in your school to observe you in your classroom and give you tips about connecting with students. Ask the superstar teacher to provide honest feedback about any students who seemed to be disconnected from you, the lesson, or the classroom, why that might be the case, and what you might do to reengage them. Inviting a colleague to observe you teach a lesson can be nerve-wracking, but remind yourself that your goal is to refine your craft and improve yourself as a teacher. By asking a trusted and valued colleague to spend time in your classroom, you will not only receive valuable feedback, but also place your colleague in the position of following Whitaker's advice to put the teacher in the students' position. Hopefully, your colleague will reciprocate and ask you to do the same, allowing you to be a student in a superstar teacher's class for a lesson.

Notes

Part Fourteen

Chapter 17: What About These Darn Standardized Tests?

🔑 Key Concepts

- Effective teachers do not allow hot-button issues to shift their focus from what really matters.

- Effective teachers do not allow standardized tests to take over the entire class, yet they work toward student success in standardized testing so it doesn't become the primary focus of the school.

- Effective teachers never allow their personal views regarding standardized testing to affect discussions they might have with their students, parents, or even peers.

- Effective teachers recognize that state standards force them to shift the focus from the textbook to the actual curriculum and student learning.

- Great teachers do not merely hold up standards and watch students make their way toward them; instead, they remain at their students' side, helping them to develop the skills they need to meet the standards.

1. What are two key questions teachers should ask in determining the role of standardized tests? What is the relationship between these two questions?

2. In the study cited in the text, what was the difference between schools that exceeded expectations on standardized tests and other schools?

3. What is a risk associated with making state standards the center of the school?

4. What things influence what is taught in any classroom? Which of these things is the single most important determinant for what happens in the classroom? Why?

5. In the matter of standardized testing—and any other potentially controversial topic—how do the most effective educators decide to deal with the issue when talking with parents, students, and peers?

Notes

Journal Prompt

At the end of the chapter, the author shares a key question he posed to teachers at a school wishing to raise its reading scores: "Are you so interested in improving your students' reading abilities that you are willing to change what you do in your classroom—or do you want to raise their test scores *so that you don't have to change* what you do in your classroom?" Write about your reaction to this question. By posing this question, what is the author hinting at in terms of what is important to teachers about standardized tests? Are most teachers willing to change what they do in their classrooms? If so, why? If not, why not? What—ultimately—should determine whether teachers change their classroom practices?

Two Key Questions

The author maintains that it is time to stop debating the merits of standardized testing and focus instead on educators' behaviors related to the issue of testing. In groups of five or less, have participants discuss the two key questions he poses: (1) What should schools be doing? (2) What do standardized tests measure? Have each group portray its answers pictorially, using a framework similar to that offered in Figure 2 on page 105 of the text. Have each group create a Top 10 list of the vitally important things that schools must do that are not measured by standardized testing. Then have each group create another Top 10 list of the most important reasons for schools to demonstrate success on standardized tests. Have groups draw their circles and write their Top 10 lists on chart paper. Ask the groups to present their findings.

The Role of Standards

This chapter notes that standards-based education is a rapidly growing movement within the larger movement of educational reform. Briefly stated, standards-based education calls for a clear identification of what students should know and be able to do. Research has shown that the amount of time spent on a specific topic can range dramatically from classroom to classroom—even at the same grade level and at the same school. The reason for this variation is, inevitably, teacher preference.

Divide participants into small groups that are clustered as closely as possible based on similar subject areas and/or grade levels. Distribute examples of clearly written performance standards currently in place at different schools. Have groups pick one subject and grade level with which all participants are comfortable. Have them examine the standards that have been distributed. Ask each group to create a simplified list of five standards that are absolutely essential areas of learning for students at that grade level. Have each group share their five standards with the entire group as a starting point for discussing the value of clearly identified critical knowledge and skills that must be learned in varying subjects at each grade level.

Notes

Application

Using Figures 1 and 2 from page 105 of the text as a guiding reference, ask five teachers and/or administrators whom you respect to answer the two questions the author poses. In addition, specifically ask these five colleagues: What things are we doing at our school that are not measured by standardized tests but are still vitally important? Are there things that the standardized tests measure that we as a school are not doing? What percentage of what we do at school is measured by standardized tests? What *should* that percentage be? What behaviors must we agree on in order to ensure success on standardized tests? Be prepared to share the feedback you receive at the next session.

Notes

Part Fifteen

Chapter 18: Make It Cool to Care
Chapter 19: Clarify Your Core

🔑 Key Concepts

- All effective teachers have a core set of beliefs to which they adhere as educators.

- Getting faculty members to go along with the latest trend or mandate has limited value; rather, the key is to develop and establish a schoolwide environment that supports everyone's efforts to do what is right.

- The real challenge—and the real accomplishment—is to get all students to care about what happens in the classroom and to create an atmosphere in which it is "cool to care."

- In great schools, the teachers tell stories about what other teachers have accomplished with students.

- Great teachers do what is right, no matter what else is going on.

- Great educators understand that behaviors and beliefs are tied to emotion, and they understand the power of emotion to jump-start change.

- Students care about great teachers because they know great teachers care about them.

- Without a core of firmly held beliefs, it is difficult for teachers to steer a steady course.

- With this core, teachers feel secure and confident. More importantly, so do their students.

- Every teacher has an impact. Great teachers make a difference.

❓ Discussion Questions

1. Why is it so important to establish a classroom environment in which it is "cool to care"?

2. What is one thing that great teachers can choose to do when colleagues make sarcastic, derogatory comments?

3. What must teachers do with students before being able to connect with their minds?

4. As a principal, why did the author decide to cease the practice of collecting lesson plans from teachers? Can you think of current or past practices that may be similar to his story?

5. What is the framework that sustains the work of all great educators?

6. Of the "17 Things That Matter Most," which do you feel is the foremost essential practice? Why?

Notes

Journal Prompt

On page 113, the author describes "The Great Teacher" he identifies as "Mrs. Heart." How did Mrs. Heart motivate Darin to become interested in poetry? What were Mrs. Heart's attitudes toward state standards, standardized tests, and new initiatives that were inevitably rolled out over the years? In your own words, what was Mrs. Heart's philosophy of education? Do you agree with this philosophy? Take a moment to describe your own philosophy of education after reading this book.

Group Activities

Seventeen Things ...

Type each of the "17 Things That Matter Most" on a separate slip of paper. Tape each item on a separate desk around the room. Arrange participants into seventeen groups (or have them work individually if there are seventeen or fewer participants). Start each group at one of the seventeen "stations" and have them spend five minutes reflecting on the item at that desk. Have them write examples from the book, or their own experience, that relate to the statement. Have them write why they feel the statement is important.

After five minutes, have each group rotate one desk (moving in numerical order, with those people at desk 17 rotating to desk 1). Repeat the process of reflecting and writing about each statement until each participant or group has moved through all seventeen stations.

Clarifying Your Core

After reviewing the author's core beliefs, ask individuals to think about additional core beliefs not mentioned in the text that are essential components of their personal mission as teachers. Have each participant write two to four additional core beliefs they value as educators. Have participants pair up to share these additional beliefs. Invite volunteers to share these with the whole group.

 Application

On page 115 of the text, Whitaker states that in great schools, teachers tell stories about the teaching legends with whom they have worked. Write about one teacher at your current school whom you consider legendary. Also write about a teacher from your own past who positively impacted you and whom you also consider a legend. Share the first story with the teacher you wrote about by placing it in that teacher's mailbox. Share the second story by mailing your account to your former teacher or to one of that person's family members.

Seventeen Things That Matter Most

1. Great teachers never forget that it is people, not programs, that determine the quality of a school.
2. Great teachers establish clear expectations at the start of the year and follow them consistently as the year progresses.
3. Great teachers manage their classrooms thoughtfully. When they say something, they mean it.
4. When a student misbehaves, great teachers have one goal: to keep that behavior from happening again.
5. Great teachers have high expectations for students but have even higher expectations for themselves.
6. Great teachers know that they are the variable in the classroom. Good teachers consistently strive to improve, and they focus on something they can control: their own performance.
7. Great teachers focus on students first, with a broad vision that keeps everything in perspective.
8. Great teachers create a positive atmosphere in their classrooms and schools. They treat every person with respect. In particular, they understand the power of praise.
9. Great teachers consistently filter out the negatives that don't matter and share a positive attitude.
10. Great teachers work hard to keep their relationships in good repair to avoid personal hurt and to repair any possible damage.
11. Great teachers have the ability to ignore trivial disturbances and the ability to respond to inappropriate behavior without escalating the situation.
12. Great teachers have a plan and purpose for everything they do. If plans don't work out the way they had envisioned, they reflect on what they could have done differently and adjust accordingly.
13. Before making any decision or attempting to bring about any change, great teachers ask themselves one central question: What will the best people think?
14. Great teachers continually ask themselves who is most comfortable and who is least comfortable with each decision they make. They treat everyone as if they were good.
15. Great teachers have empathy for students and clarity about how others see them.
16. Great teachers keep standardized testing in perspective. They focus on the real issue of student learning.
17. Great teachers care about their students. They understand that behaviors and beliefs are tied to emotion, and they understand the power of emotion to jump-start change.